African-American Excellence
In Pursuit of the Dream

Compiled by :
Millie Mackiney

Cover Illustration by Design Dynamics

Published by Great Quotations, Inc.
Glendale Heights, IL

Library of Congress Catalog number: 99-072988
ISBN: 1-56245-391-2

Printed In Hong Kong

Introduction:

Collected from scholars and leaders; poets and scientists; actors, activists and athletes; this chorus of inspired words reflects and defines the standards of African-American excellence, in pursuit of the dream.

3

I Dream a World

I dream a world where man
no other will scorn,
where love will bless the earth
and peace its paths adorn.
I dream a world where all
will know sweet freedom's
way,
where greed no longer
saps the soul
nor avarice blights our day.
a world I dream where
Black or White,
whatever race you be,

will share the bounties of
the earth
and every man is free.
where wretchedness will
hang its head
and joy, like a pearl,
attend the needs of all
mankind.
Of such I dream -
our world!

Langston Hughes

Excellence is not an act but a habit. The things you do the most are the things you do the best.

Marva Collins

A dream doesn't become
reality through magic; it
takes sweat, determination
and hard work.

General Colin L. Powell

I used to want the words,
"She tried" on my
tombstone. Now I want,
"She did it."

Katherine Dunham

The more you praise and celebrate your life, the more there is in life to celebrate.

Oprah Winfrey

A good head and a good heart are always a formidable combination.

Nelson Mandela

He who is not courageous
enough to take risks will
accomplish nothing in life.

Muhammad Ali

I try to do the right thing at the right time. They may just be little things, but usually they make the difference between winning and losing.

Kareem Abdul Jabbar

How far you go in life depends on your being tender with the young, compassionate with the aged, sympathetic with the striving, and tolerant of the weak and strong. Because someday in life you will have been all of these.

George Washington Carver

Light has come into the world,
and every man must decide
whether he will walk in the
light of creative altruism or
the darkness of destructive
selfishness.

Dr. Martin Luther King, Jr.

14

Friends are my heart and my ears.

Michael Jordan

Anytime you see someone more successful than you are, they are doing something that you aren't.

Malcolm X

The most worthwhile endeavor I have ever undertaken is responsibility for my own life. It's hard, and it's worth it.

LeVar Burton

If a man hasn't discovered something he will die for, he isn't fit to live.

Dr. Martin Luther King, Jr.

Let our opportunities
overshadow our grievances.

Booker T. Washington

You have to expect things of yourself before you can do them.

Michael Jordan

Let nothing and nobody break your spirit.

Jesse L. Jackson

We are one, our cause is one, and we must help each other if we are to succeed.

Frederick Douglass

But for ourselves, who know our plight too well, there is a need of great patterns to guide us, great lives to inspire us, strong men and women to lift us up and give us confidence in the powers we, too, possess.

Langston Hughes

Everything that we see is a shadow cast by that which we do not see.

Dr. Martin Luther King, Jr.

We make our living by what
we get. We make our life by
what we give.

Benjamin E. Mays

Blacks and Whites must meet and know each other as brothers in a marriage of visions, as co-conspirators in the making of a dream, as fellow passengers on a journey into the unknown.

Lerone Bennett, Jr.

You have to know that your real home is within.

Quincy Jones

We can't rely on anyone but ourselves to define our existence, to shape the image of ourselves.

Spike Lee

We get close to God as we get more acquainted with the things He has created. I know of nothing more inspiring than that of making discoveries for one's self.

George Washington Carver

Black Americans must begin to accept a larger share of responsibility for their lives...To fight any battle takes soldiers who are strong, healthy, committed, well trained, and confident.

Jesse L. Jackson

If you have a purpose in which you can believe, there's no end to the amount of things you can accomplish.

Marian Anderson

You have to KNOW you can win.

"Sugar" Ray Leonard

The guy who takes a chance, who walks the line between the known and the unknown, who is unafraid of failure, will succeed.

Gordon Parks

Since we live in a changing universe, why do men oppose change? If a rock is in the way, the root of a tree will change its direction.

Melvin Tolson

Even the smallest victory is never to be taken for granted. Each victory must be applauded, because it is so easy not to battle at all, to just accept and call that acceptance inevitable.

Audre Lorde

35

My family directly and my people indirectly have given me the kind of strength that enables me to go anywhere.

Maya Angelou

Though it is sometimes very difficult to imagine our nation totally free of racism and sexism, my intellect, my heart and my experience tell me that it is actually possible. For that day when neither exists we must all struggle.

James Baldwin

Surely people of good will come together to salvage the world.

Betty Shabazz

The potential for strength, endurance, courage, inventiveness, and creativity exists in every human being God created.

Michelle Wallace

The thing I have done throughout my life is to do the best job that I can do to be me.

Mae Jemison

Presumption should never make us neglect that which appears easy to us, nor despair make us lose courage at the sight of difficulties.

Benjamin Banneker

There are roads out of the secret places within us along which we all must move as we go to touch others.

Romare Bearden

The measure of a country's greatness is its ability to retain compassion in times of crisis.

Thurgood Marshall

We must turn to each other
and not on each other.

Jesse L. Jackson

In our ethnic and racial diversity, we are all brothers and sisters in a quest for greatness.

Harold Washington

I am a product of every other Black woman before me who has done or said anything worthwhile. Recognizing that I am a part of that history is what allows me to soar.

Oprah Winfrey

We grew up in a generation
where people were concerned
about what you were going to
be, because the race needed
you. We were reared to
believe a single failure was
one that we could not afford.
I hope we can regain that
urgency.

Bishop Leontine Kelly

One of the new terms is *Role Model*. When people do not want to do what history requires, they say they have no role model. I'm glad Phyllis Wheatley did not know she had no role model and wrote her poetry anyway. I'm glad Harriet Tubman did not know she had no role model and led the slaves to freedom.

I'm glad that Frederick Douglass did not know he had no role model and walked off that plantation to become one of the great oratorical fighters for freedom.

Nikki Giovanni

I always had only one prayer, "Lord, just crack the door a little bit, and I'll kick it open all the way."

Shirley Caesar

Whatever reason you had for not being somebody, there's somebody who had that same problem and overcame it.

Barbara Reynolds

I have learned to take "NO" as a vitamin.

Suzanne de Passe

Opportunity follows struggle.
It follows effort. It follows
hard work. It doesn't come
before.

Shelby Steele

When times get tough, rejoice in the knowledge that you are one in a long line of proud, courageous people who have a history of surviving.

Denise L. Stinson

The image you have of
yourself is important. If you
feel like a failure, chances are
you'll fail. If you think you'll
succeed, you'll be successful.
You can't just sit back and
expect people to do things for
you. You've got to get up
and do it yourself.

Diana Ross

Your world is as big as you make it.

Georgia Douglas Johnson

I never said, "I don't have this and I don't have that". I said, "I don't have this yet, but I'm going to get it.

Tina Turner

I think people like Julius
Erving, Denzel Washington,
Spike Lee, and Martin Luther
King- people I admire- all
created their own vision...they
set an example and they led.
But you don't have to be on
television, coach an NBA
team, or play a professional
sport to

be an effective leader. Just about every home, every business, every neighborhood and every family needs someone to lead it. We've got enough people talking about it.

Michael Jordan

I think that education is power. I think that being able to communicate with people is power. I do think that the greatest lesson of life is that you are responsible for your own life.

Oprah Winfrey

Education is our passport to the future, for tomorrow belongs to the people who prepare for it today.

Malcolm X

According to the commonest principles of human action, no man will do as much for you as you will do for yourself.

Marcus Garvey

GOD makes three requests of His children: Do the best you can, where you are, with what you have now.

African American Proverb

I had to make my own living
and my own opportunity.
Don't sit down and wait for
the opportunities to come; you
have to get up and make them.

Madame C. J. Walker

If you do what you've always done, you'll get what you've always gotten.

Jackie "Moms" Mabley

The greatest thing I ever was able to do was give a welfare check back. I brought it back and said, "Here, I don't need this anymore."

Whoopi Goldberg

There's a lot of talk about self esteem these days. It seems pretty basic to me. If you want to feel good about yourself, you've got to do things that you can be proud of.

Osceola McCarty

I've always been driven, but I'm not the kind of person who says, "This is going to take me here, and that's going to take me here." I don't have goals - I have standards of achievement.

Ed Bradley

The way to be successful is through preparation. It doesn't just happen. You don't wake up one morning and discover you're a lawyer any more than you wake up as a pro football player. It takes time.

Alan Page

We all have ability - the
difference is in how we use it.

Stevie Wonder

At the bottom of education, at the bottom of politics, even at the bottom of religion, there must be economic independence.

Booker T. Washington

Money has no color. If you can build a better mousetrap, it won't matter whether you're Black or White, people will buy it.

A. G. Gaston

Defining myself, as opposed to being defined by others, is one of the most difficult challenges I face.

Carol Moseley Braun

We create our own destiny by the way we do things. We have to take advantage of opportunities and be responsible for our choices.

Benjamin Carson

There is a great wisdom in the message of self reliance, education, of hard work, and of the need to raise strong families.

General Colin L. Powell

Invest in the human soul-who knows, it just might be a diamond in the rough.

Mary McLeod Bethune

I act as if everything depends
on me and pray as if
everything depends on GOD.

Oprah Winfrey

There are no secrets to success: Don't waste time looking for them. Success is the result of perfection, hard work, learning from failure, loyalty to those for whom you work, and persistence.

General Colin L. Powell

Other Titles by Great Quotations, Inc

Hard Covers

African American Excellence
Ancient Echoes
Attitudes of Success
Behold the Golfer
Celebrating Friendship
Commanders In Chief
Dare to Dream
First Ladies
Graduation
Golf
Good Lies for Ladies
Heartfelt Affection
Improving With Age
Inspirations for Success
Inspired Thoughts
I Thought of You Today
Journey to Success
Just Between Friends
Keys to Achieving Your Goals

Lasting Impressions
My Dear Mom
My Husband, My Love
Never Ever Give Up
Peace Be With You
Seeds of Inspiration
Seeds of Knowledge
Sharing Our Love
Sharing the Season
Smile Now
Teddy Bears
The Essence of Music
The Passion of Chocolate
The Perfect Brew
The Power of Inspiration
There's No Place Like Home
The Spirit of Christmas
Thoughts From Great Women

Great Quotations, Inc.
1967 Quincy Court
Glendale Heights, IL 60139 USA
Phone: 630-582-2800 Fax: 630-582-2813
http://www. greatquotations.com

Other Titles by Great Quotations, Inc

Paperbacks

A Servant's Heart
A Teacher is Better Than Two Books
I'm Not Over the Hill
Life's Lessons
Looking for Mr. Right
Midwest Wisdom
Mommy & Me
Mother, I Love You
Motivating Quotes
Mrs. Murphy's Laws
Mrs. Webster's Dictionary
Only A Sister
Parenting 101
Pink Power
Romantic Rhapsody
Social Disgraces
Stress or Sanity
The Mother Load
The Other Species
The Secret Langauge of Men
The Secret Langauge of Women
The Secrets in Your Name
Teenage of Insanity
Touch of Friendship
Wedding Wonders
Words From the Coach

Perpetual Calendars

365 Reasons to Eat Chocolate
All Star Quotes
Always Remember Who Loves You
A Touch of Kindness
Coffee Breaks
Extraordinary Leaders
Generations
I'm a Little Stressed
I Think My Teacher Sleeps at School
Kid Stuff
My Friend & Me
Never Never Give Up
Older Than Dirt
Secrets of a Successful Mom
Shopoholic
Sweet Dreams
Teacher Zone
Tee Times
The Dog Ate My Car Keys
The Essence of Great Women
The Heart That Loves
The Honey Jar
Winning Words